Coloring in English

CAT

A Vocabulary Builder for Beginners

Tracy Speelman

PRO LINGUA ⬤ ASSOCIATES

D1451793

Contents: the Topics

Pro Lingua Associates
PO Box 1348, Brattleboro, Vermont 05302
www.ProLinguaAssociates.com
orders@ProLinguaAssociates.com
800-366-4775 • 802-267-7779

Coloring in English was designed by Arthur A. Burrows. It was set in *Futura*, a sans-serif face developed in 1927 by Paul Renner and in *Tahoma*, developed in 1994 by Matthew Carter for Microsoft. *Tempus Sans ITC* is the display font, developed in 1996 by Phill Grimshaw. Back cover photo © Ximagination Dreamstime Agency

The book was printed and bound by Royal Palm Press in Punta Gorda, Florida.

Printed in the United States of America

Second printing 2015.

Notes
to the teacher

Coloring in English is intended for basic literacy and/or beginning ESL learners of all ages. It works best as a low-pressure, fun activity. Adults and children can relax and color as they learn new vocabulary and important sight words.

Most of the pages are repeated side-by-side, usually as "mirror images" with FULL CAPS on one side and Upper and Lower Case print on the other. The learners can color whatever appeals to them, all or part of either picture, or both. They will naturally compare the words in full caps with those not in caps.

There are a few "extra" pictures and inconsistencies in format added for fun and to encourage questions.

I hope your students have as much fun coloring these pages in English as my editors and I have had putting this book together.

Tracy Speelman

PETS

FISH

SNAKE

HAMSTER

TAIL

PAW

RABBIT

COLLAR

BIRD

CAT

DOG

BIRD	CAT	COLLAR	DOG	FISH
HAMSTER	PAW	RABBIT	SNAKE	TAIL

Pets

snake

fish

hamster

tail

paw

rabbit

bird

collar

cat

dog

bird	cat	collar	dog	fish
hamster	paw	rabbit	snake	tail

3

FARM ANIMALS

CHICKEN

GOOSE

DUCK

TURKEY

SHEEP

GOAT

PIG

DONKEY

HORSE

COW

CHICKEN	COW	DONKEY	DUCK	GOAT
GOOSE	HORSE	PIG	SHEEP	TURKEY

Farm Animals

chicken	cow	donkey	duck	goat
goose	horse	pig	sheep	turkey

5

WILD ANIMALS

TIGER

LION

MONKEY

GIRAFFE

PANDA

ZEBRA

GORILLA

DEER

ELEPHANT

BEAR

BEAR	DEER	ELEPHANT	GIRAFFE	GORILLA
LION	MONKEY	PANDA	TIGER	ZEBRA

Wild Animals

tiger

lion

monkey

panda

giraffe

zebra

gorilla

deer

elephant

bear

bear	deer	elephant	giraffe	gorilla
lion	monkey	panda	tiger	zebra

SEA ANIMALS

DOLPHIN

SWORDFISH

WHALE

SEA LION

CLAM

STARFISH

SEA HORSE

PENGUIN

SEAL

WALRUS

CLAM	DOLPHIN	PENGUIN	SEA HORSE	SEA LION
SEAL	STARFISH	SWORDFISH	WALRUS	WHALE

Sea Animals

dolphin

swordfish

whale

sea lion

penguin

sea horse

starfish

clam

seal

walrus

clam	dolphin	penguin	sea horse	sea lion
seal	starfish	swordfish	walrus	whale

BACKYARD NATURE

	ANT	BEE	BIRD	BUTTERFLY	FLOWER
10	FROG	SPIDER	SQUIRREL	TREE	WORM

Backyard Nature

squirrel

bird

tree

flower

spider

butterfly

frog

worm

bee

inchworm

ant

ant	bee	bird	butterfly	flower
frog	spider	squirrel	tree	worm

11

HOUSE

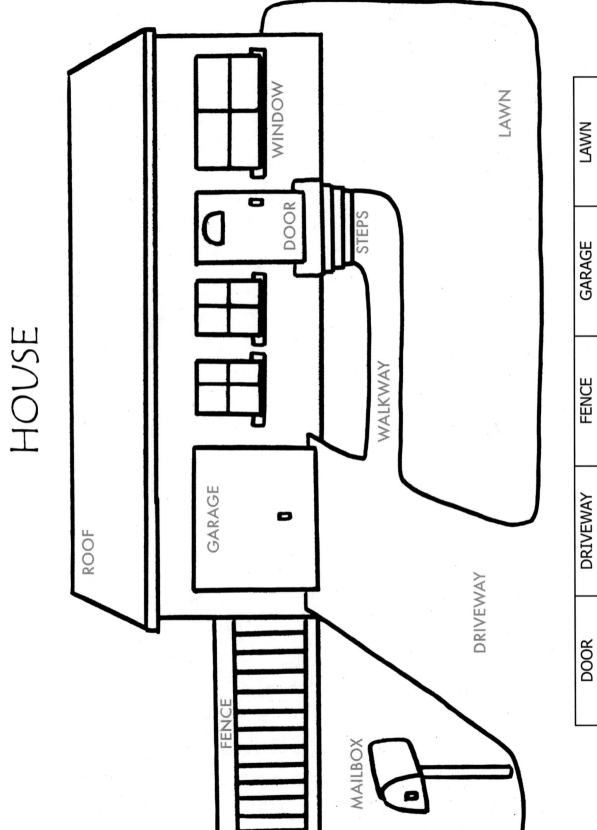

ROOF

WINDOW

DOOR

GARAGE

STEPS

WALKWAY

FENCE

MAILBOX

DRIVEWAY

LAWN

DOOR	DRIVEWAY	FENCE	GARAGE	LAWN
MAILBOX	ROOF	STEPS	WALKWAY	WINDOW

House

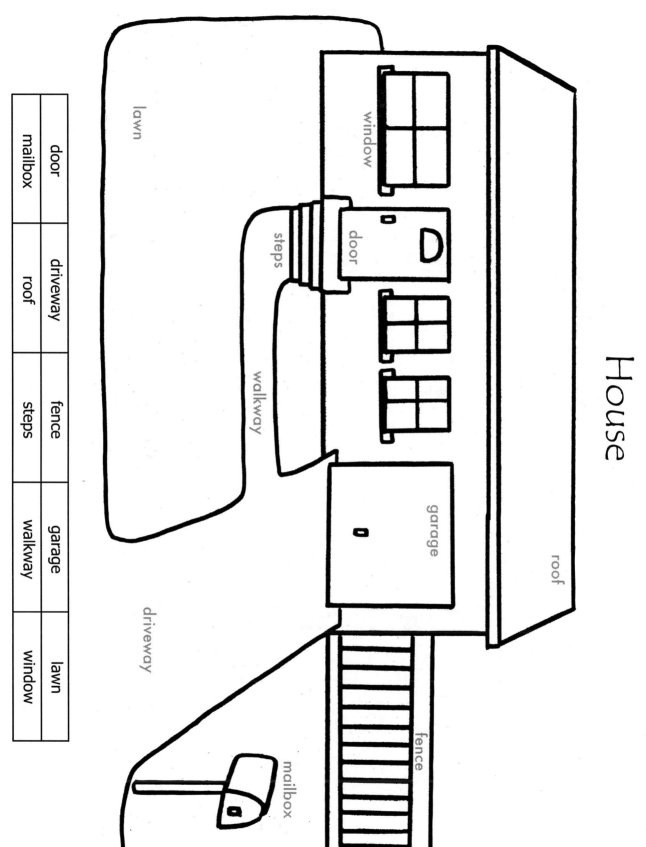

door	mailbox
driveway	roof
fence	steps
garage	walkway
lawn	window

7

LIVING ROOM

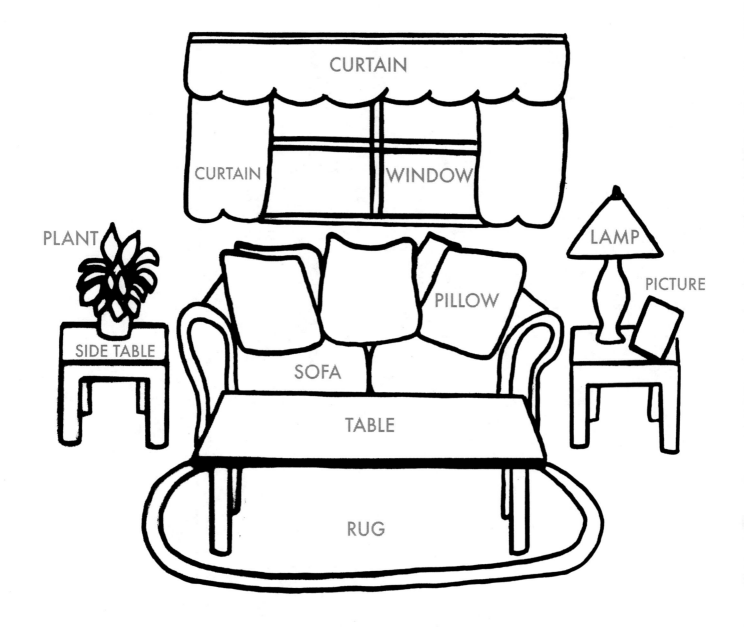

CURTAIN	LAMP	PICTURE	PILLOW	PLANT
RUG	SIDE TABLE	SOFA	TABLE	WINDOW

14

Living Room

curtain	lamp	picture	pillow	plant
rug	side table	sofa	table	window

BEDROOM

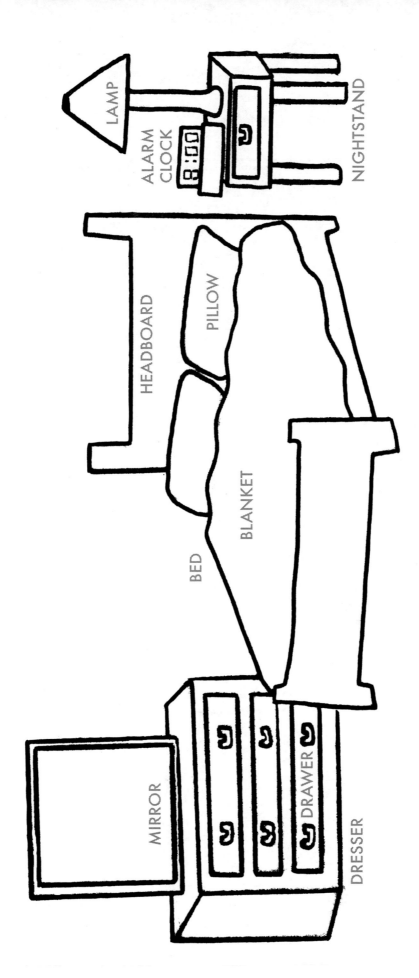

ALARM CLOCK	BED	BLANKET	DRAWER	DRESSER
HEADBOARD	LAMP	MIRROR	NIGHTSTAND	PILLOW

Bedroom

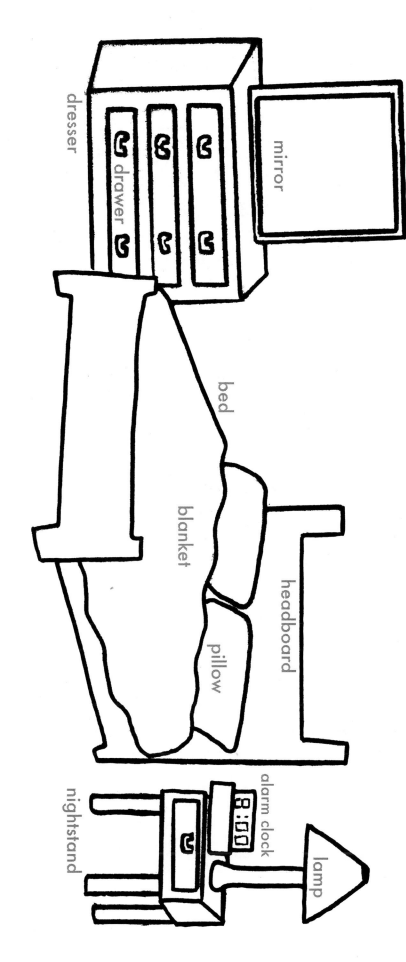

alarm clock	bed	blanket	drawer	dresser
headboard	lamp	mirror	nightstand	pillow

BATHROOM

TOOTHPASTE

TOOTHBRUSH ↘

SOAP

SINK

WASTE BASKET

SCALE

TOILET

TOILET PAPER

PLUNGER

BATHTUB

BATHTUB	PLUNGER	SCALE	SINK	SOAP
TOILET	TOILET PAPER	TOOTHBRUSH	TOOTHPASTE	WASTE BASKET

Bathroom

soap

toothpaste

toothbrush

sink

waste basket

scale

toilet

toilet paper

plunger

bathtub

bathtub	plunger	scale	sink	soap
toilet	toilet paper	toothbrush	toothpaste	waste basket

19

KITCHEN

SINK

TEA POT

TOASTER

DISHWASHER

MICROWAVE

POT HOLDER

STOVE

CABINET

OVEN

REFRIGERATOR

CABINET	DISHWASHER	MICROWAVE	OVEN	POT HOLDER
REFRIGERATOR	SINK	STOVE	TEA POT	TOASTER

Kitchen

tea pot

sink

dishwasher

toaster

pot holder

microwave

stove

oven

refrigerator

cabinet

cabinet	dishwasher	microwave	oven	pot holder
refrigerator	sink	stove	tea pot	toaster

21

KITCHEN THINGS

WHISK

LADLE

PIZZA CUTTER

SPATULA

CAN OPENER

KITCHEN KNIFE

PEELER

SAUCE PAN

CASSEROLE

FRYING PAN

CAN OPENER	CASSEROLE	FRYING PAN	KITCHEN KNIFE	LADLE
PEELER	PIZZA CUTTER	SAUCE PAN	SPATULA	WHISK

Kitchen Things

pizza cutter

ladle

whisk

can opener

spatula

kitchen knife

peeler

sauce pan

casserole

frying pan

can opener	casserole	frying pan	kitchen knife	ladle
peeler	pizza cutter	sauce pan	spatula	whisk

23

TABLE SETTING

BOWL

SUGARBOWL

GLASS

SALT S P PEPPER

KNIFE

MUG

FORK

SPOON

PLATE

NAPKIN

BOWL	FORK	GLASS	KNIFE	MUG
NAPKIN	PLATE	SALT AND PEPPER	SPOON	SUGARBOWL

Table Setting

glass

sugarbowl

bowl

salt

S

P

pepper

mug

knife

fork

spoon

plate

Napkin

bowl	fork	glass	knife	mug
napkin	plate	salt and pepper	spoon	sugarbowl

25

CONTAINERS

BOTTLE

ENVELOPE

CAN

BOX

BAG

BASKET

TUBE

JAR

JUG

BIN

BAG	BASKET	BIN	BOTTLE	BOX
CAN	ENVELOPE	JAR	JUG	TUBE

Containers

bag	basket	bin	bottle	box
can	envelope	jar	jug	tube

27

CLEANING SUPPLIES

DUST PAN

WHISK BROOM

SPONGE

DUSTER

SPRAY BOTTLE

MOP

BROOM

CARPET SWEEPER

VACUUM

BUCKET

CARPET SWEEPER	BROOM	BUCKET	DUST PAN	DUSTER
MOP	SPONGE	SPRAY BOTTLE	VACUUM	WHISK BROOM

Cleaning Supplies

sponge

whisk broom

dust pan

spray bottle

duster

carpet sweeper

mop

broom

vacuum

bucket

carpet sweeper	broom	bucket	dust pan	duster
mop	sponge	spray bottle	vacuum	whisk broom

LAUNDRY

IRONING BOARD

IRON

BASKET

CLOTHES LINE

HANGER

CLOTHES PIN

WASHER

DRYER

DETERGENT

HAMPER

BASKET	CLOTHES LINE	CLOTHES PIN	DETERGENT	DRYER
HAMPER	HANGER	IRON	IRONING BOARD	WASHER

Laundry

basket

iron

ironing board

clothes line

clothes pin

hanger

detergent

hamper

dryer

washer

basket	clothes line	clothes pin	detergent	dryer
hamper	hanger	iron	ironing board	washer

TOOLS

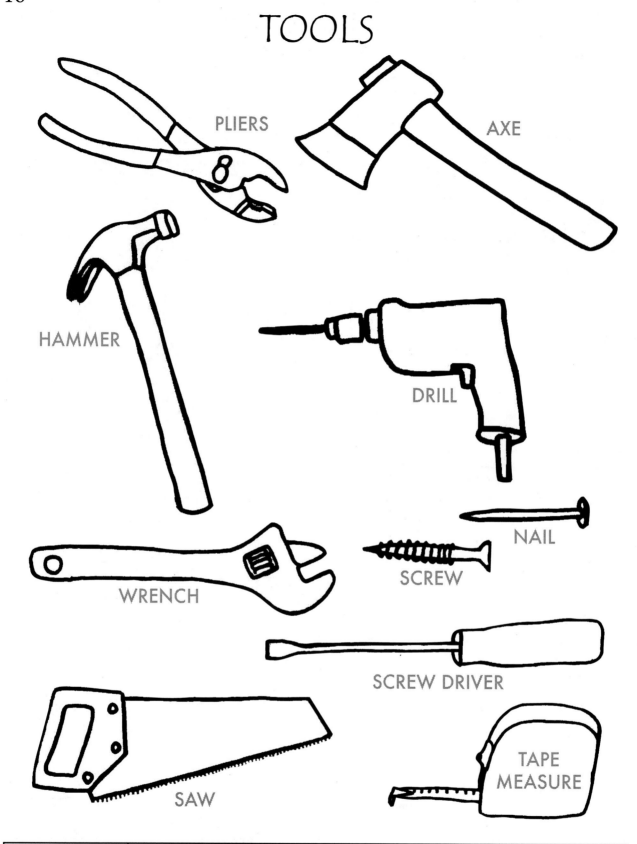

PLIERS

AXE

HAMMER

DRILL

NAIL

WRENCH

SCREW

SCREW DRIVER

SAW

TAPE MEASURE

	AXE	DRILL	HAMMER	NAIL	PLIERS
32	SAW	SCREW	SCREW DRIVER	TAPE MEASURE	WRENCH

Tools

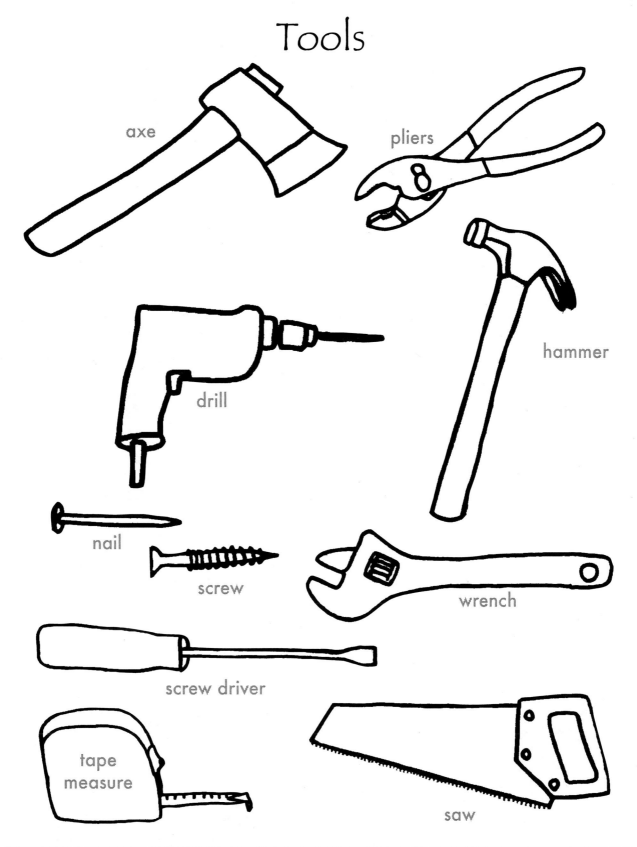

axe

pliers

hammer

drill

nail

screw

wrench

screw driver

tape measure

saw

axe	drill	hammer	nail	pliers
saw	screw	screw driver	tape measure	wrench

33

VEGETABLES

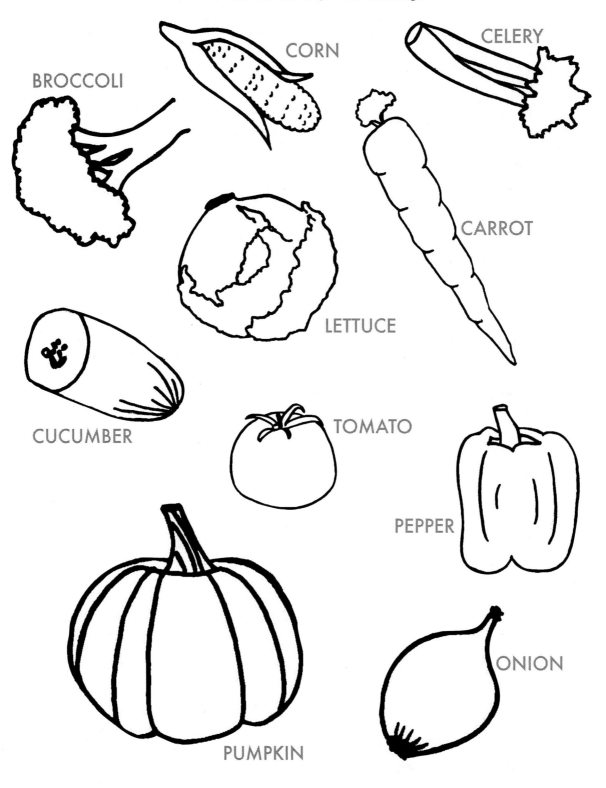

CORN

CELERY

BROCCOLI

CARROT

LETTUCE

CUCUMBER

TOMATO

PEPPER

PUMPKIN

ONION

BROCCOLI	CARROT	CELERY	CORN	CUCUMBER
LETTUCE	ONION	PEPPER	PUMPKIN	TOMATO

Vegetables

celery

corn

broccoli

carrot

lettuce

cucumber

tomato

pepper

onion

pumpkin

broccoli	carrot	celery	corn	cucumber
lettuce	onion	pepper	pumpkin	tomato

35

FRUIT

APPLE

ORANGE

BANANA

CHERRY

STRAWBERRY

LEMON

PEAR

PINEAPPLE

WATERMELON

GRAPES

APPLE	BANANA	CHERRY	GRAPES	LEMON
ORANGE	PEAR	PINEAPPLE	STRAWBERRY	WATERMELON

Fruit

apple

banana

orange

strawberry

cherry

pineapple

pear

lemon

watermelon

grapes

apple	banana	cherry	grapes	lemon
orange	pear	pineapple	strawberry	watermelon

37

BODY

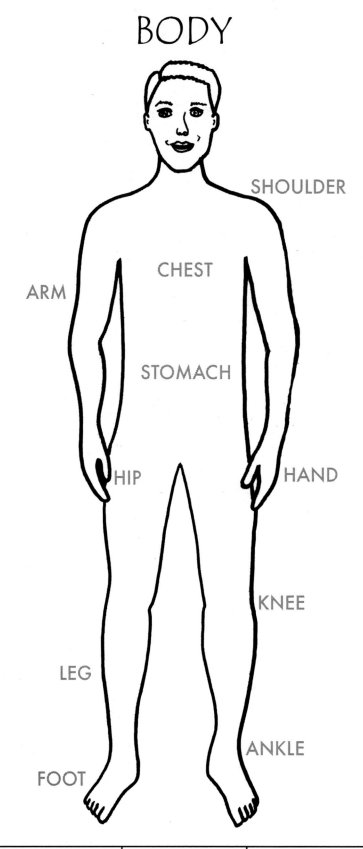

SHOULDER

CHEST

ARM

STOMACH

HIP

HAND

KNEE

LEG

ANKLE

FOOT

ANKLE	ARM	CHEST	FOOT	HAND
HIP	KNEE	LEG	SHOULDER	STOMACH

Body

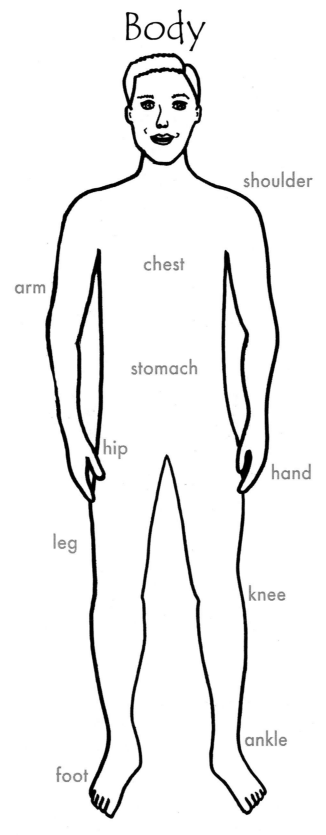

shoulder

chest

arm

stomach

hip

hand

leg

knee

ankle

foot

ankle	arm	chest	foot	hand
hip	knee	leg	shoulder	stomach

39

FACE

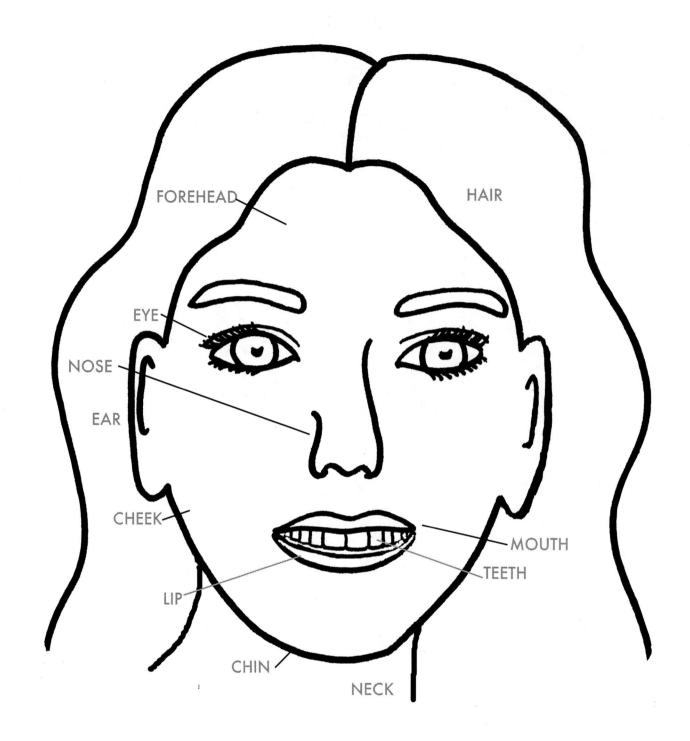

FOREHEAD

HAIR

EYE

NOSE

EAR

CHEEK

MOUTH

TEETH

LIP

CHIN

NECK

CHEEK	CHIN	EAR	EYE	FOREHEAD
LIP	MOUTH	NECK	NOSE	TEETH

Face

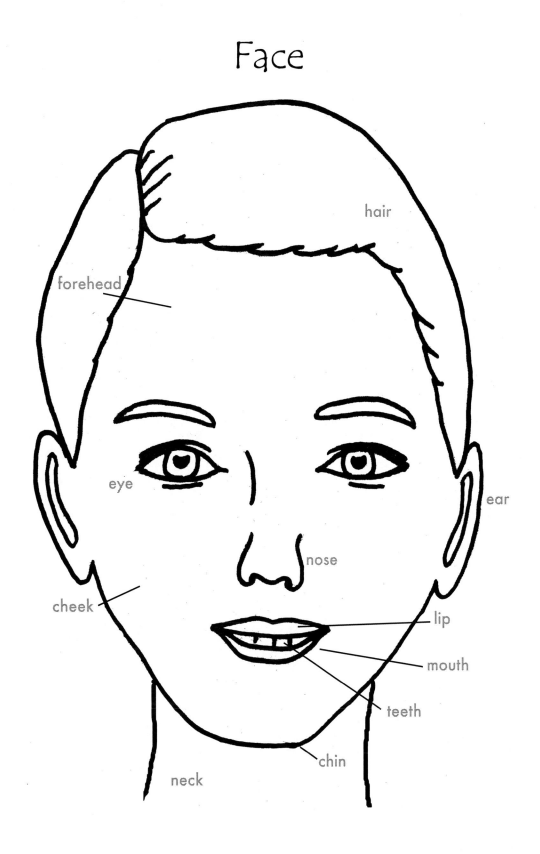

cheek	chin	ear	eye	forehead
hair	lip	mouth	nose	neck

41

HAND AND FOOT

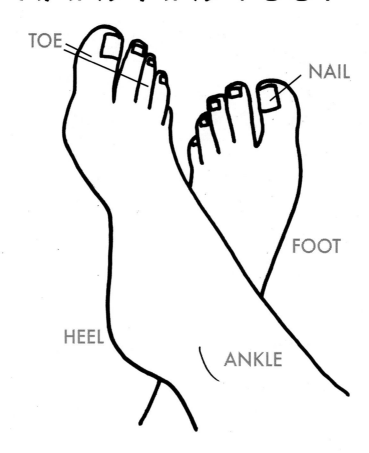

TOE

NAIL

FOOT

HEEL

ANKLE

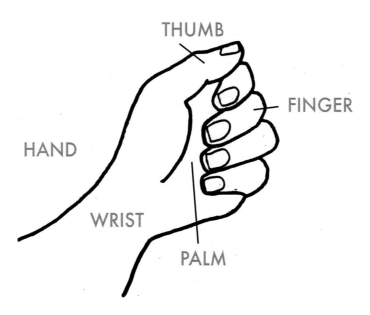

THUMB

FINGER

HAND

WRIST

PALM

	ANKLE	FINGER	FOOT	HAND	HEEL
42	NAIL	PALM	THUMB	TOE	WRIST

Hand and Foot

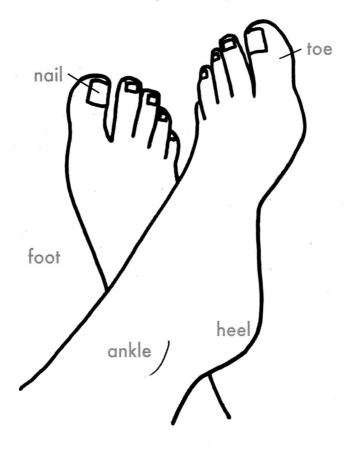

nail

toe

foot

ankle

heel

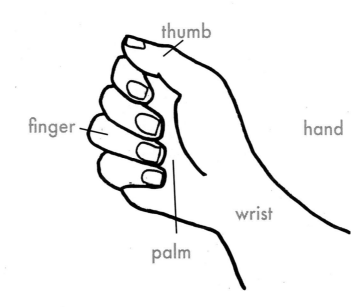

thumb

finger

hand

palm

wrist

ankle	finger	foot	hand	heel
nail	palm	thumb	toe	wrist

43

CLOTHES

CAP

JACKET

TEE SHIRT

SHIRT

SHORTS

DRESS

PANTS

SOCKS

SKIRT

SHOE

CAP	DRESS	JACKET	PANTS	SHIRT
SHOE	SHORTS	SKIRT	SOCKS	TEE SHIRT

Clothes

cap

shirt

tee shirt

jacket

shorts

pants

dress

socks

shoe

skirt

cap	dress	jacket	pants	shirt
shoe	shorts	skirt	socks	tee shirt

45

ACCESSORIES

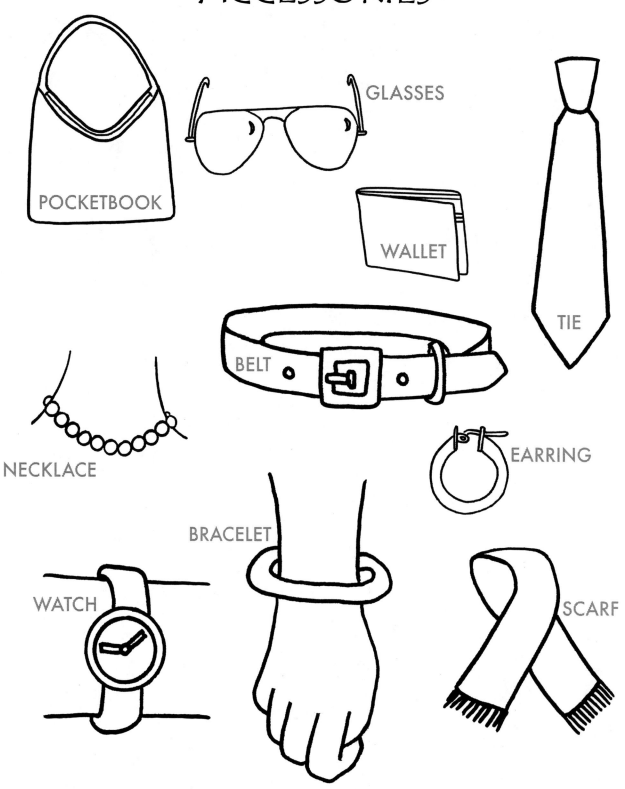

POCKETBOOK

GLASSES

WALLET

TIE

BELT

NECKLACE

EARRING

BRACELET

WATCH

SCARF

BELT	BRACELET	EARRING	GLASSES	NECKLACE
POCKETBOOK	SCARF	TIE	WALLET	WATCH

Accessories

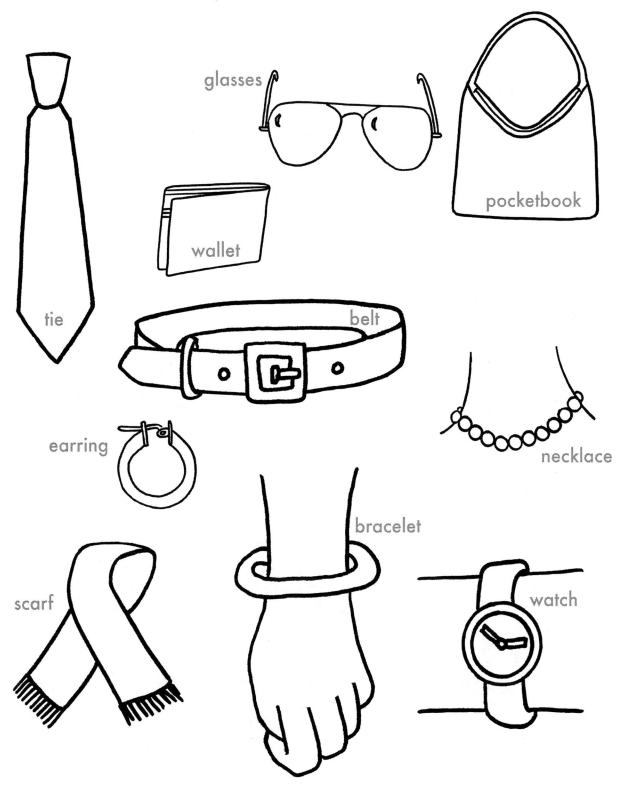

glasses

pocketbook

wallet

tie

belt

earring

necklace

bracelet

scarf

watch

belt	bracelet	earring	glasses	necklace
pocketbook	scarf	tie	wallet	watch

WINTER

GLOVES

MITTENS

COAT

SNOWMAN

HAT

EARMUFFS

SKATE

BOOTS

SKIS

SLED

	BOOTS	COAT	EARMUFFS	GLOVES	HAT
48	MITTENS	SKATE	SKIS	SLED	SNOWMAN

Winter

gloves

mittens

snowman

coat

skate

earmuffs

hat

skis

sled

boots

boots	coat	earmuffs	gloves	hat
mittens	skate	skis	sled	snowman

49

SUMMER

BEACH HAT

BATHING SUIT

SUNGLASSES

KITE

UMBRELLA

SUN SCREEN

BEACH BALL

PAIL AND
SHOVEL

BARBEQUE

BEACH CHAIR

BARBEQUE	BATHING SUIT	BEACH BALL	BEACH CHAIR	BEACH HAT
KITE	PAIL AND SHOVEL	SUNGLASSES	SUN SCREEN	UMBRELLA

50

Summer

kite

sunglasses

beach hat

bathing suit

sun screen

umbrella

beach ball

barbeque

pail and shovel

beach chair

barbeque	bathing suit	beach ball	beach chair	beach hat
kite	pail and shovel	sunglasses	sun screen	umbrella

51

ON THE STREET

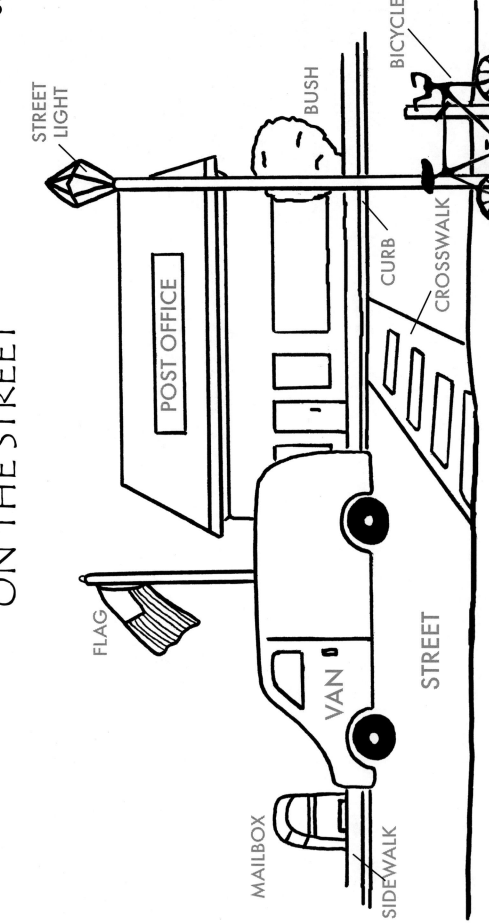

STREET
LIGHT

BICYCLE

BUSH

POST OFFICE

CURB

CROSSWALK

FLAG

VAN

STREET

MAILBOX

SIDEWALK

BICYCLE	BUSH	CROSSWALK	CURB	FLAG
MAILBOX	POST OFFICE	SIDEWALK	STREET	VAN

On the Street

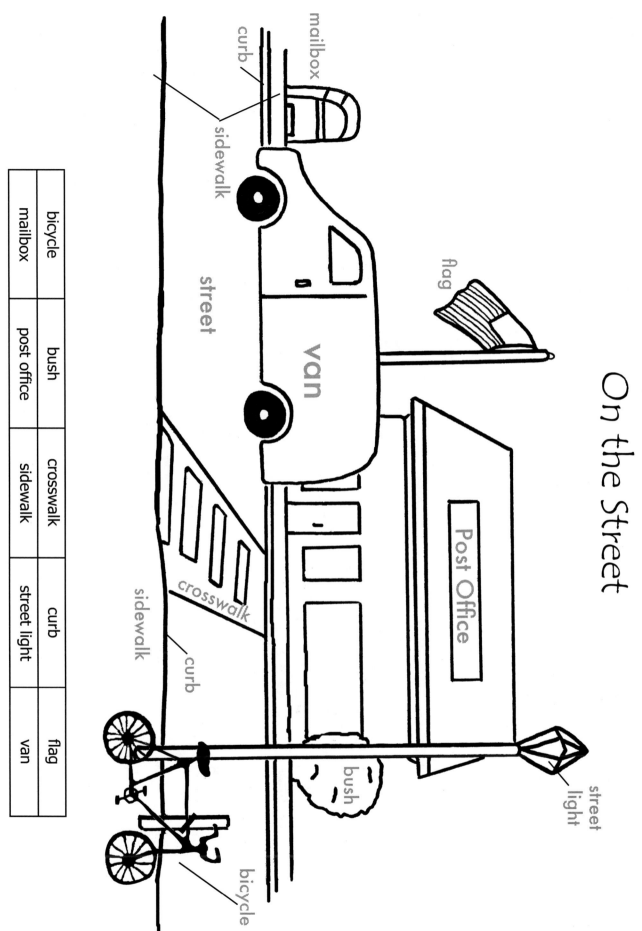

bicycle	bush	crosswalk	curb	flag
mailbox	post office	sidewalk	street light	van

53

STREET SIGNS

RED/STOP

YELLOW/YIELD

GREEN/GO

STREET LIGHT

DEER CROSSING

SPEED LIMIT 55

STOP

DO NOT ENTER

YIELD

ONE WAY

DEER CROSSING	DO NOT ENTER	ONE WAY	SPEED LIMIT	STOP
STREET LIGHT	YIELD	RED/STOP	YELLOW/YIELD	GREEN/GO

Street Signs

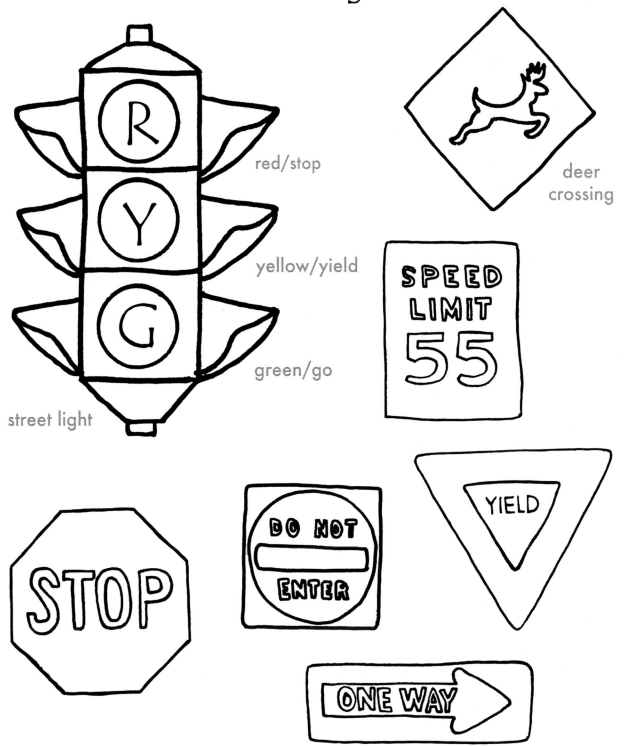

red/stop

yellow/yield

green/go

street light

deer crossing

SPEED LIMIT 55

DO NOT ENTER

YIELD

STOP

ONE WAY

deer crossing	do not enter	one way	speed limit	stop
street light	yield	red/stop	yellow/yield	green/go

55

TRANSPORTATION

SCHOOL BUS

AIRPLANE

AMBULANCE

HELICOPTER

BUS

TRUCK

TAXI

CAR

TRAIN

LIMOUSINE

AIRPLANE	AMBULANCE	BUS	CAR	HELICOPTER
LIMOUSINE	SCHOOL BUS	TAXI	TRAIN	TRUCK

Transportation

airplane

school bus

ambulance

bus

helicopter

truck

car

taxi

train

limousine

airplane	ambulance	bus	car	helicopter
limousine	school bus	taxi	train	truck

57

CAR EXTERIOR

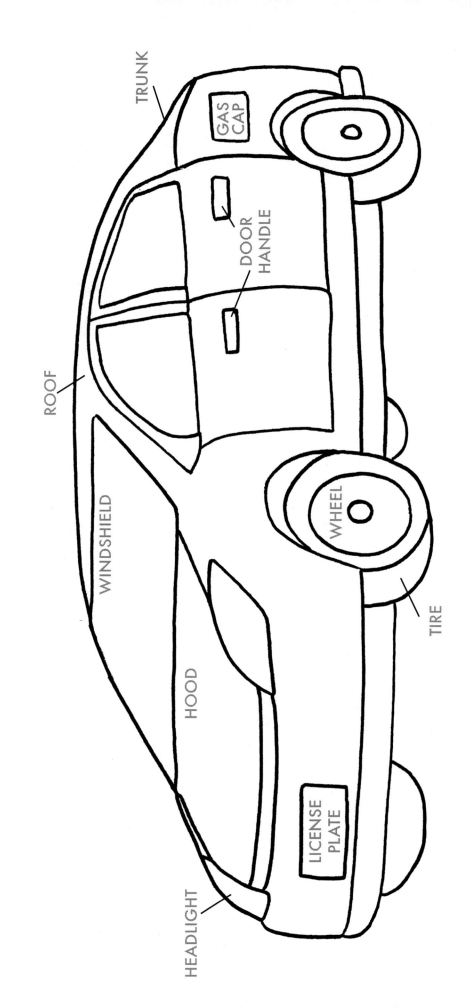

DOOR HANDLE	GAS CAP	HEADLIGHT	HOOD	LICENSE PLATE
ROOF	TIRE	TRUNK	WHEEL	WINDSHIELD

Car Exterior

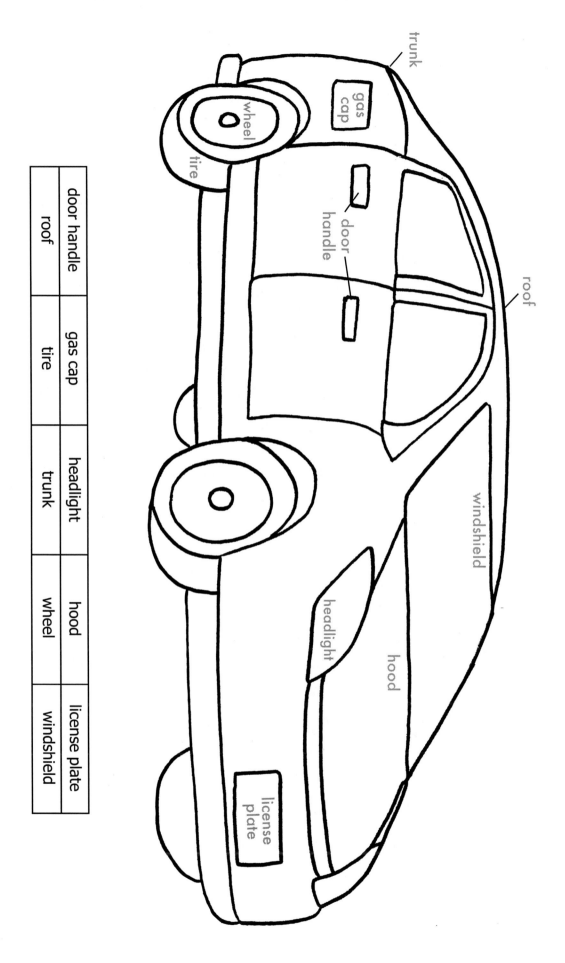

door handle	roof	tire	trunk	windshield
gas cap	headlight	trunk	wheel	license plate

Labels on image: trunk, gas cap, wheel, tire, door handle, roof, windshield, headlight, hood, license plate

30

CAR INTERIOR

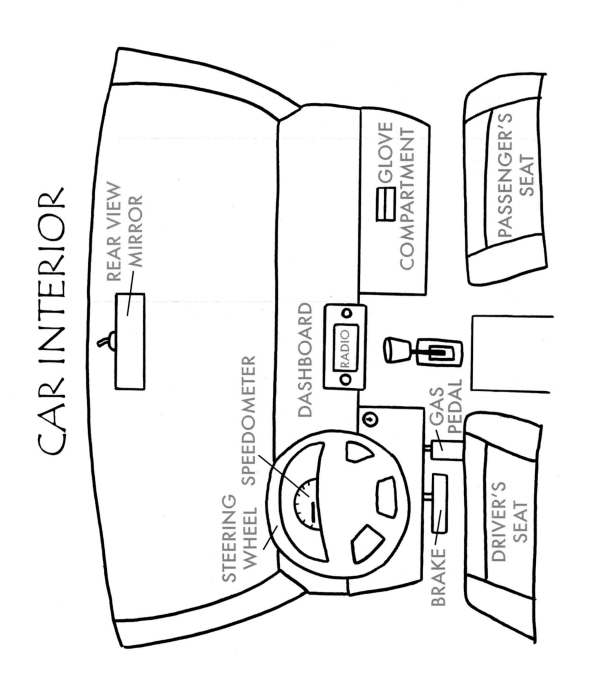

REAR VIEW MIRROR

STEERING WHEEL

SPEEDOMETER

DASHBOARD

RADIO

GLOVE COMPARTMENT

GAS PEDAL

BRAKE

DRIVER'S SEAT

PASSENGER'S SEAT

BRAKE	DASHBOARD	DRIVER'S SEAT	GAS PEDAL	GLOVE COMPARTMENT
PASSENGER'S SEAT	RADIO	REAR VIEW MIRROR	SPEEDOMETER	STEERING WHEEL

Car Interior

brake	dashboard	driver's seat	rear view mirror	speedometer	glove compartment
passenger's seat	radio	driver's seat	speedometer	gas pedal	steering wheel

steering wheel

brake

driver's seat

speedometer

gas pedal

dashboard

radio

glove compartment

passenger's seat

rear view mirror

31

CLASSROOM

CHAIR

DESK

PENCIL

NOTEBOOK

BOARD

2 + 3 = 5

LAPTOP

READING

BOOK

PEN

MARKER

BOARD	BOOK	CHAIR	DESK	LAPTOP
MARKER	NOTEBOOK	PEN	PENCIL	READING

Classroom

desk

chair

pencil

$2 + 3 = 5$

board

notebook

laptop

reading

book

pen

marker

board	book	chair	desk	laptop
marker	notebook	pen	pencil	reading

SPORTS

BAT

BASEBALL

BASKETBALL

BASKETBALL NET

HOCKEY STICK

FOOTBALL HELMET

FOOTBALL

PUCK

SOCCERBALL

SOCCER GOAL

BASEBALL	BASKETBALL	BASKETBALL NET	BAT	FOOTBALL
FOOTBALL HELMET	HOCKEY STICK	PUCK	SOCCERBALL	SOCCER GOAL

Sports

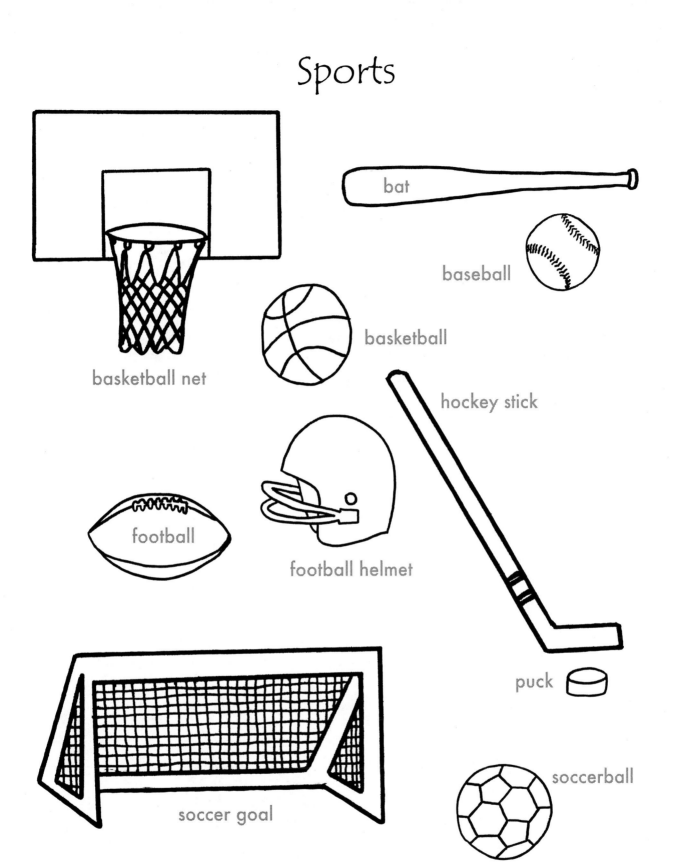

bat

baseball

basketball

basketball net

hockey stick

football

football helmet

puck

soccer goal

soccerball

baseball	basketball	basketball net	bat	football
football helmet	hockey stick	puck	soccerball	soccer goal

65

33

WEATHER

SUN

RAIN

SNOW

MOON

UMBRELLA

CLOUD

HOT

COLD

LIGHTNING

FAN

RAINBOW

CLOUD	COLD	HOT	LIGHTNING	MOON
SNOW	SUN	RAIN	RAINBOW	UMBRELLA

Weather

snow

rain

sun

cloud

umbrella

moon

lightning

cold

hot

rainbow

fan

cloud	cold	hot	lightning	moon
snow	sun	rain	rainbow	umbrella

FISHING AT THE LAKE

BOAT	DOCK	FISHERMAN	GRASS	LAKE
MOUNTAIN	STREAM	TREE	WATERFALL	WOODS

34

68

Fishing at the Lake

boat	dock	fisherman	grass	lake
mountain	stream	tree	waterfall	woods

69

CAMPING IN THE WOODS

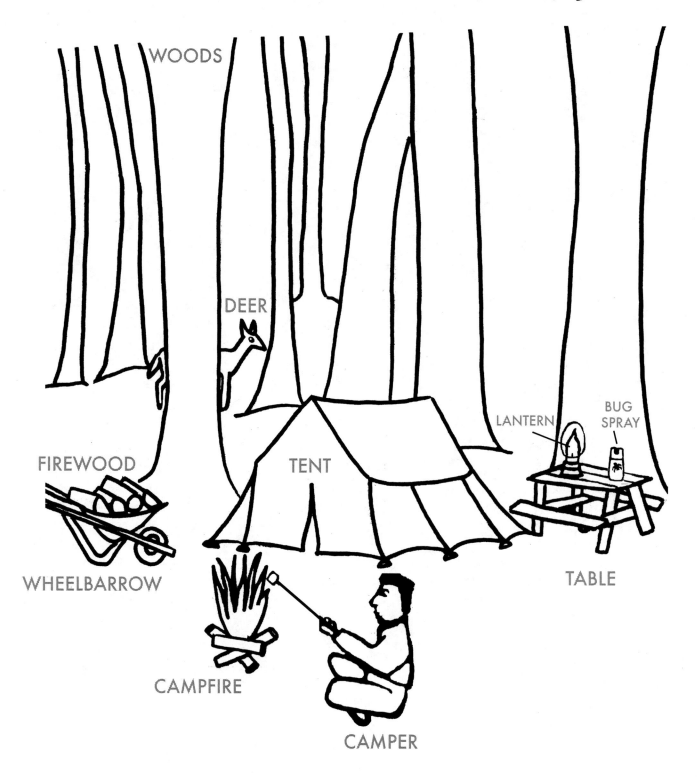

WOODS

DEER

LANTERN

BUG SPRAY

FIREWOOD

TENT

WHEELBARROW

TABLE

CAMPFIRE

CAMPER

BUG SPRAY	CAMPER	CAMPFIRE	DEER	FIREWOOD
LANTERN	TABLE	TENT	WHEELBARROW	WOODS

Camping in the Woods

woods

bug spray

lantern

tent

deer

firewood

table

wheelbarrow

campfire

camper

bug spray	camper	campfire	deer	firewood
lantern	table	tent	wheelbarrow	woods

71

OFFICE

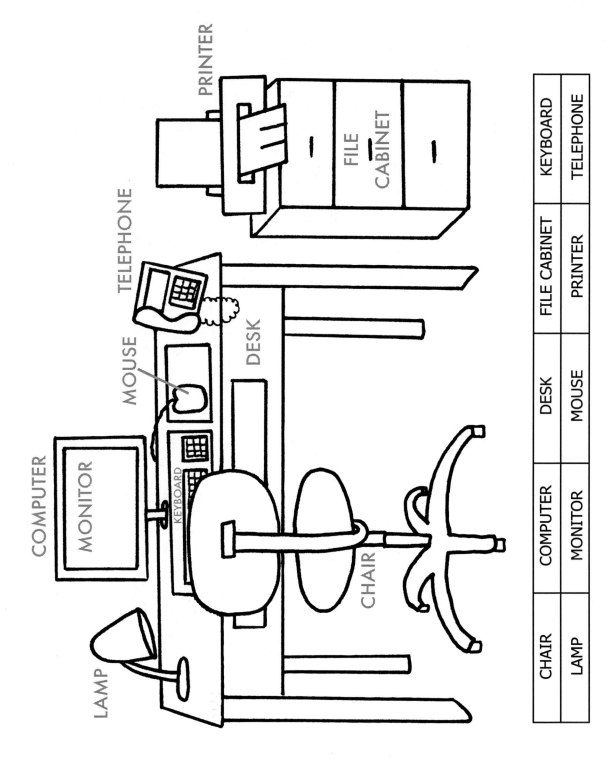

CHAIR	COMPUTER	DESK	FILE CABINET	KEYBOARD
LAMP	MONITOR	MOUSE	PRINTER	TELEPHONE

Office

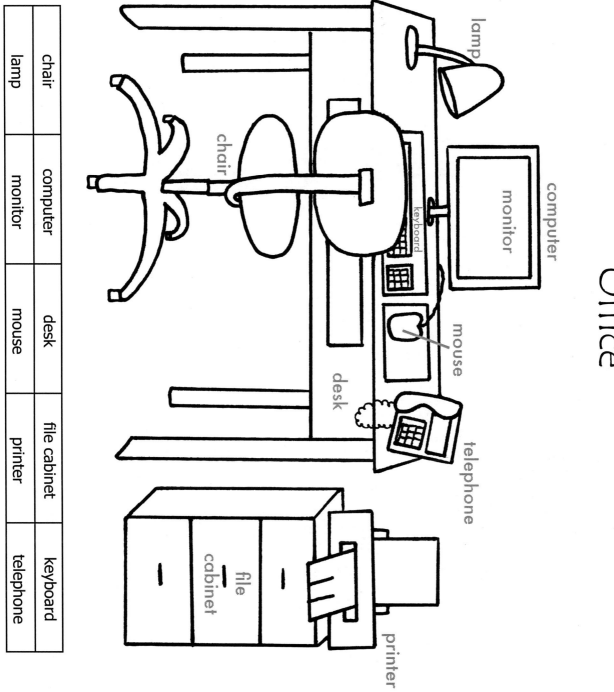

chair	computer	desk	file cabinet	keyboard
lamp	monitor	mouse	printer	telephone

73

37

OFFICE SUPPLIES

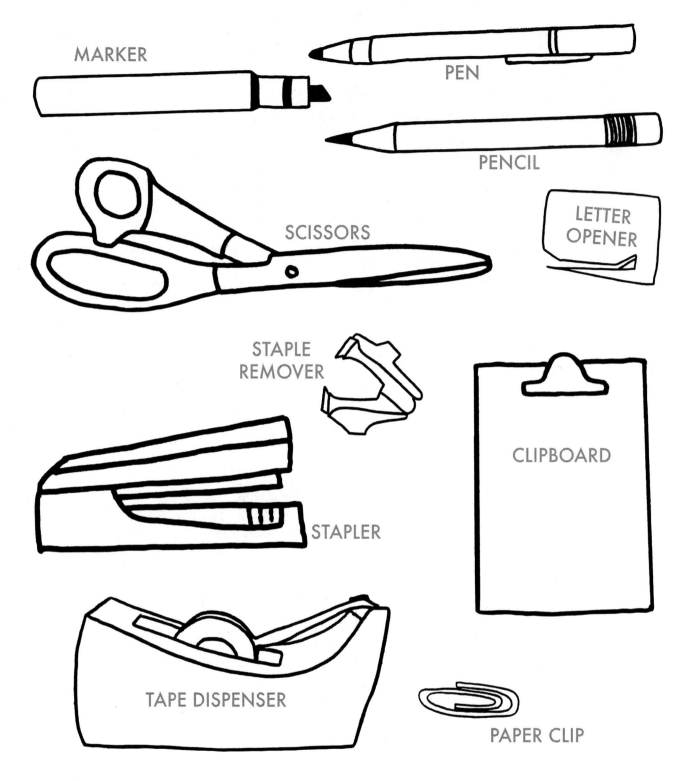

MARKER

PEN

PENCIL

SCISSORS

LETTER OPENER

STAPLE REMOVER

CLIPBOARD

STAPLER

TAPE DISPENSER

PAPER CLIP

CLIPBOARD	LETTER OPENER	MARKER	PAPER CLIP	PEN
PENCIL	SCISSORS	STAPLE REMOVER	STAPLER	TAPE DISPENSER

Office Supplies

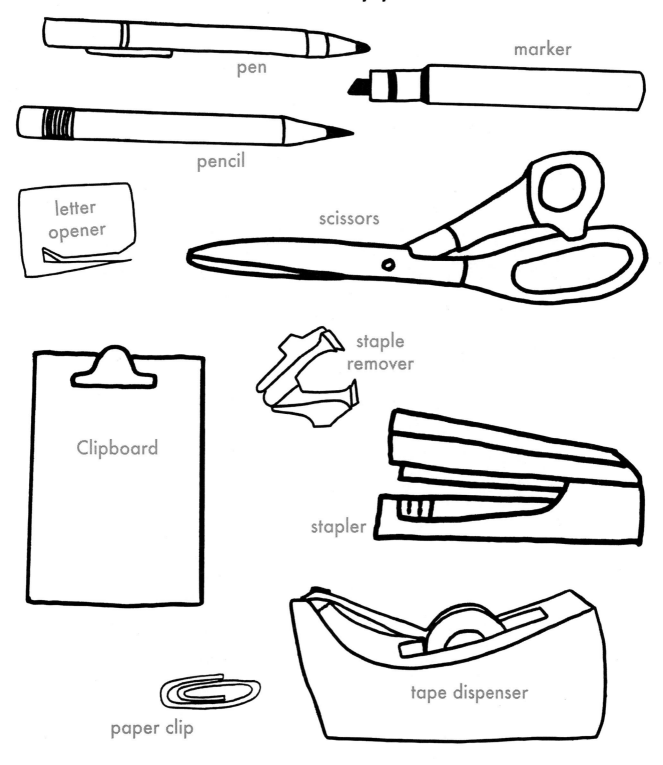

pen

marker

pencil

letter opener

scissors

staple remover

Clipboard

stapler

paper clip

tape dispenser

clipboard	letter opener	marker	paper clip	pen
pencil	scissors	staple remover	stapler	tape dispenser

VERBS – COMMUNICATION

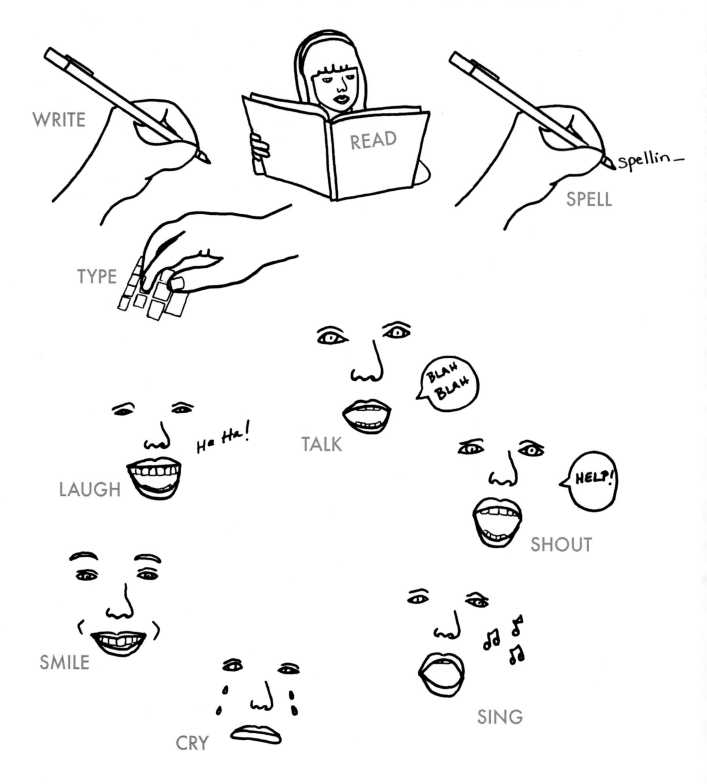

WRITE

READ

SPELL

spellin–

TYPE

TALK

BLAH BLAH

Ha Ha!

LAUGH

HELP!

SHOUT

SMILE

SING

CRY

CRY	LAUGH	READ	SHOUT	SING
SMILE	SPELL	TALK	TYPE	WRITE

VERBS – ACTION

WALK   RUN   JUMP   SIT   PLAY

EAT

DRINK

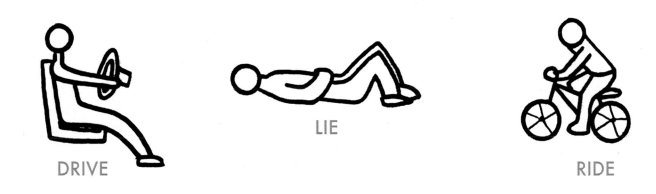

DRIVE   LIE   RIDE

DRINK	DRIVE	EAT	JUMP	LIE
PLAY	RIDE	RUN	SIT	WALK

NUMBERS

ONE – 1

TWO – 2

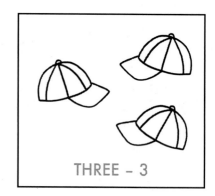

THREE – 3

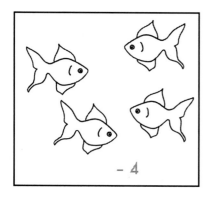

– 4

– 5

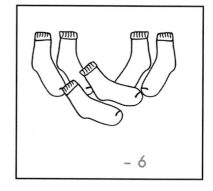

– 6

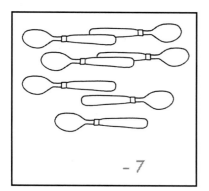

– 7

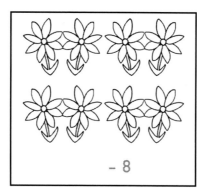

– 8

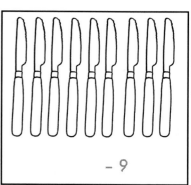

– 9

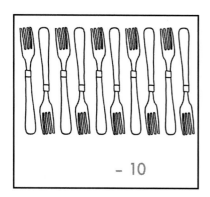

– 10

ELEVEN– 11

TWELVE– 12

ONE – 1	TWO – 2	THREE – 3	FOUR – 4	FIVE – 5
SIX – 6	SEVEN – 7	EIGHT – 8	NINE – 9	TEN – 10